W9-BDJ-869

EDGE
BOOKS™

INFECTED!

CHOLERA

HOW THE BLUE DEATH CHANGED HISTORY

by Mark L. Lewis

Consultant

Sean Moore, PhD
Research Assistant Professor, Biology
University of Notre Dame

CAPSTONE PRESS
a capstone imprint

Edge Books are published by Capstone Press,
1710 Roe Crest Drive, North Mankato, Minnesota 56003
www.mycapstone.com

Library of Congress Cataloging-in-Publication Data
Names: Lewis, Mark L., 1991–author.
Title: Cholera : how the blue death changed history / Mark L. Lewis.
Description: North Mankato, Minnesota : Capstone Press, 2020 | Series:
  Infected! | Audience: Grades 4 to 6. | Includes bibliographical references
  and index.
Identifiers: LCCN 2018061088 (print) | LCCN 2019000501 (ebook) | ISBN
  9781543572421 (ebook) | ISBN 9781543572384 (hardcover)
Subjects: LCSH: Cholera—Juvenile literature. | Cholera—History—Juvenile
  literature. | Cholera—Prevention—Juvenile literature. |
  Epidemics—History—Juvenile literature. | Diseases and history—Juvenile
  literature.
Classification: LCC RC126 (ebook) | LCC RC126 .L54 2020 (print) | DDC 616.9/32
LC record available at https://lccn.loc.gov/2018061088

All internet sites appearing in back matter were available and accurate when this book
was sent to press.

Editorial Credits
Editor: Megan Ellis
Designer: Craig Hinton
Production Specialist: Craig Hinton

Photo Credits
Alamy: Photo12/Ann Ronan Picture Library, 12, Pictorial Press Ltd, 13; Centers for Disease Control
and Prevention: Benjamin Dahl, Ph.D., M.P.H./Molly Kurnit, M.P.H./Public Health Image Library, 26,
Public Health Image Library, 5, 29; Getty Images: Paula Bronstein/Getty Images News, 21; iStockphoto:
imagestock, 8, ktsimage, 16, Rawpixel, 9; Library of Congress: Bain News Service/George Grantham
Bain Collection, 17; Science Source: Dr P. Marazzi, 6, Jim Dowdalls, 10–11, Mark Edwards/UIG, 27;
Shutterstock Images: Authentic Travel, 7, hagit berkovich, 14–15, John Wollwerth, cover (bottom),
Kateryna Kon, cover (top), 1, Kekyalyaynen, 24–25, kittirat roekburi, 18, Oshchepkov Dmitry, 20, Scott
Woodham Photography, 23

Design Elements
Shutterstock Images

Printed in the United States of America.
PA70

TABLE OF CONTENTS

CHAPTER 1

INFECTED RIVERS IN KENYA

In July 2017, Rasoa Lutenyi could not stop vomiting in her home in Nairobi, Kenya. If she tried to eat something, she vomited it back up immediately. She also had severe diarrhea. It was watery and gray. It looked like water that had been used to boil rice.

Her sister took her to the hospital to figure out what was wrong. Doctors put her on an **intravenous** (IV) drip. She was very **dehydrated**. Her body had lost a lot of water trying to get rid of the illness as fast as possible. The "rice water" color of the diarrhea came from cells in her intestines. These cells came out of Lutenyi's body while it tried to remove the illness.

intravenous—given through the veins
dehydrated—a state of not having enough water

Doctors did tests and scans to figure out what was making Lutenyi sick. They diagnosed her with cholera.

WHAT IS CHOLERA?

Cholera is a **bacterium**. There are two types of cholera bacteria that affect humans.

Cholera symptoms include diarrhea, nausea, and vomiting. This leads to dehydration. Someone with cholera can lose up to 34 ounces (1 liter) of water per hour from his or her body. A person may become irritable and confused or have dry, cracked skin. Severe dehydration also causes muscle cramps and **shock**. If left untreated, cholera can lead to death.

bacterium—a tiny organism that can cause illness
shock—a medical condition caused by a dangerous drop in blood pressure and flow; people suffering from shock can die

Unfortunately, Lutenyi's body was too dehydrated to recover from cholera. Lutenyi died in the hospital three days later. Lutenyi was not the only person with cholera in Nairobi. The cholera **epidemic** in Nairobi had begun in December 2016. Three hundred people went to the hospital because of cholera. Six people died.

CONTAINING AN OUTBREAK

In 2017 Kenyan authorities worked quickly to contain the cholera outbreak. The bacteria spread through **contaminated** water sources. These sources can reach hundreds of people in just a few hours. People who lived outside of the city often did not have enough resources to deal with a cholera outbreak. Organizations such as UNICEF and the Red Cross helped. They fixed broken pipes that allowed bacteria to contaminate the water.

epidemic—an outbreak of a disease that covers multiple cities
contaminated—unfit for use because of contact with a harmful substance

Local authorities also made sure water was safe to drink. They tested the water in rivers and lakes. They also tested the water that people sold. Some hotels and restaurants closed because the water was infected. Leaders were able to stop the spread of the disease. However, cholera is still **endemic** to Kenya. Cholera is a problem around the world. Researchers estimate that up to 140,000 people die from cholera every year.

Cholera spreads quickly through areas where people live close together and use the same sources of water.

FAST FACT

Cholera used to be called the blue death because it causes patients' skin to turn a bluish color.

endemic—regularly found in a certain area

CHOLERA'S EARLY HISTORY

Cholera is an ancient disease. The Greek physician Hippocrates wrote about a disease resembling cholera in the 300s BC. Other historians and doctors wrote about instances of cholera outbreaks over the next few centuries.

Hippocrates (left) is considered the father of modern medicine.

A WORLDWIDE DISEASE

In the past 200 years, there have been seven cholera **pandemics**. Cholera can spread rapidly as people move from city to city and country to country. The first recorded pandemic started in India in 1817.

8 pandemic—a worldwide outbreak of an infectious disease

Cholera spread quickly because of contaminated rice. Cholera bacteria can live for a long time in bodies of water such as rivers and lakes. As it rains, rivers carry the bacteria through cities. The bacteria can also soak into grains such as rice. Rice is an important crop in India. Many people ate contaminated rice.

FAST FACT

So many people died during a cholera epidemic in 1543 that a town in India had trouble burying everyone.

Rice grows in watery fields called paddies.

Cholera spread to other countries when people traveled. Bacteria live in the intestines for up to 10 days. Cholera leaves the body through human feces. Feces can then enter other waterways. Travelers along trade routes spread the disease quickly. Soldiers from Great Britain and Nepal were also carriers of cholera. People also carried cholera into southeast Asia and then into southern Europe.

People were surprised by how quickly cholera spread. No one knew how to stop it. The pandemic lasted for six years. Scientists say it was likely stopped because of a harsh winter. Cold weather may have killed the bacteria.

Cholera bacteria live in intestines. Humans absorb nutrients through their intestines.

FAST FACT

People in the United States sold fake cures for cholera in the 1800s.

For several years there were no large cholera pandemics. But in 1829, a second pandemic began. The disease arrived in Great Britain for the first time. In 1831 it arrived in North America as Irish farmers moved to the United States. That year there were 700 outbreaks across Europe, Asia, and Africa. By 1833 the disease was in Mexico and Cuba. This cholera pandemic lasted for 20 years.

Another pandemic started in 1852. Researchers believe it was the deadliest. Between 1852 and 1859, cholera spread throughout most of the world. Despite important scientific discoveries about the spread of cholera, more than 1 million people died.

CHAPTER 3

FINDING A CAUSE

Outbreaks in London, England, during the 1800s caused widespread panic. People were afraid of cholera because they did not know much about it. Many doctors believed cholera spread through the air. Others thought cholera was caused by miasmas. Miasmas were poisonous gases. One treatment in 1819 was for an infected person to wear a wool belt around the stomach. This was thought to help with the stomach pain and stop diarrhea.

Cholera spread quickly in London, England, because people lived close together.

FAST FACT

Doctors believed that miasmas rose from sewers and garbage dumps.

EPIDEMIOLOGY

John Snow was one of the first people to figure out how cholera spread. He is considered the father of modern epidemiology. Epidemiology is the study of how a disease spreads through a population.

In 1849 John Snow published a paper. He did not agree that cholera was spread through the air. Snow believed that cholera was spread through eating or drinking. Snow developed this **hypothesis** by looking at patients with cholera. He studied their symptoms. Snow believed that if cholera was airborne, victims would have trouble breathing. However, symptoms included diarrhea and vomiting. Snow thought people were becoming infected through food or water.

John Snow helped trace cholera sources in London.

hypothesis—an educated guess that can be tested

Snow proved his hypothesis in 1854. He studied maps of areas in London. He looked at where the water supply came from. He found that a single water pump was the source of most cases of cholera. When he presented his findings to the authorities, they didn't believe him at first. They removed the pump handle as a precaution. Immediately, cases of cholera dropped.

EPIDEMIOLOGY METHODS

It took several years for people to believe Snow's theory. But his techniques for mapping a disease are still used today. Snow went from door to door asking people questions about their daily lives. He compared the water sources for each household. Snow then looked at which households had people who contracted cholera.

Snow created a map to see where the water sources overlapped. This led him to discover the water pump. Snow's method is simple but effective.

Epidemiologists look for **trends**. They ask questions about what people have in common with one another. Today scientists collect information about groups of people. They collect data differently. Researchers can take body scans and blood samples.

Some communities use group water pumps instead of indoor plumbing.

FAST FACT

Not all people who contract cholera show symptoms. But they can still spread the disease.

trend—a pattern in data

CHAPTER 4

FIGHTING BACTERIA

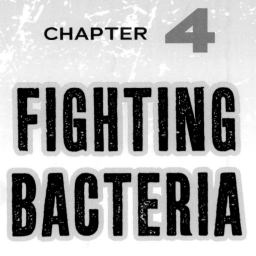

Despite Snow's research on how cholera spread, it was not widely known what caused cholera. Some scientists thought it might be caused by tiny organisms. But no one had been able to prove it.

THE FINDINGS OF ROBERT KOCH

Robert Koch was a scientist who grew up in Germany. Infectious diseases fascinated him. Koch carried out many experiments. He proved that all infections were caused by different **microorganisms**. This led him to study cholera. Koch wanted to discover what was causing the pandemics.

microorganism—a tiny organism that can only be seen through a microscope

When a cholera epidemic hit Egypt, Koch went to the country to study the disease. He thought the infection was caused by a certain type of bacteria. It was called vibrio bacteria. A vibrio bacteria cell is comma-shaped. This shape helps it move quickly in the water. It also helps the bacteria spread.

FAST FACT

An Italian scientist, Filippo Pacini, found the comma-shaped bacteria before Koch. He published a paper about cholera in 1854. Koch and Pacini did not know about each other's work.

Vibrio cells can move quickly because of their curved shape.

After the epidemic ended in Egypt, Koch traveled to India. While he was there, he continued his cholera research. Koch found a type of bacteria in the intestines of people with cholera. But he could not prove that the bacteria caused cholera.

Koch had a hypothesis that if he could **isolate** the bacteria, he could look for it in other cholera patients. To do this, Koch separated different bacteria cells in a sample from someone with cholera. Koch confirmed that the comma-shaped bacteria were present in all cholera patients. He also proved that cholera was spread through eating and drinking contaminated food and water, as Snow had earlier stated.

Robert Koch won a Nobel Prize for his research on bacteria and diseases.

isolate—to separate from something else

Robert Koch changed the way that scientists studied bacteria. His methods of growing and controlling microorganisms in a lab are still used today.

Scientists today isolate bacteria in laboratories.

FAST FACT

Medical workers often diagnose cholera by finding the bacteria in a sample of the patient's feces. In countries without access to laboratory equipment, any patient with severe, watery diarrhea is diagnosed with cholera.

DEVELOPMENT OF A VACCINE

Once Koch discovered the cholera bacteria, researchers worked to create a **vaccine**. Scientist Jaime Ferrán tested a cholera vaccine in 1884. Ferrán worked with bacteria that could still infect people. These bacteria were live versions. He gave the vaccine to 50,000 people. However, the bacteria were too strong. Many people got sick and died.

In 1892 Russian scientist Waldemar Mordecai Haffkine developed the first successful cholera vaccine. The bacteria were grown in a laboratory. They were then injected into a guinea pig and harvested. This process happened 20 times before the bacteria were weak enough. Haffkine's vaccine was not very effective. But it did protect some people from cholera.

To make a safe vaccine, Haffkine weakened cholera bacteria by injecting them into a guinea pig.

vaccine—a substance made up of dead, weakened, or living organisms that is given to a person to protect against a disease

LIVE BACTERIA VACCINES

Some vaccines, such as the influenza vaccine, use versions of the virus or bacteria that are dead. Others, such as Haffkine's cholera vaccine, use versions that are alive but weakened. Scientists use live bacteria in vaccines for many reasons. One reason is that vaccines using live bacteria can be more effective.

Several new vaccines have been created since Haffkine's vaccine. They are more effective at preventing cholera. Scientists continue to develop more effective versions of cholera vaccines.

One version of the cholera vaccine is taken orally.

PREVENTING AND TREATING CHOLERA

Even though a cholera vaccine exists, the disease affects much of sub-Saharan Africa and southern Asia every year. Researchers are trying to find solutions for these areas to end cholera.

ROADBLOCKS TO PREVENTION

Many people affected by cholera rely heavily on nearby rivers. These water sources provide people with drinking water. However, people also bathe in these rivers. If one person has cholera, the water can become infected. Rivers easily spread bacteria downstream. This can impact other areas.

Cholera bacteria spread through unclean water sources. This water is then used by people who live nearby for cooking, cleaning, and drinking.

The most effective way for people to avoid cholera is to wash their hands with soap and clean water. It is also important to dispose of human waste safely. Then it does not get into the drinking water. Many people know that it is important to wash their hands after using the bathroom. But not every person does it.

FAST FACT

In 2016 the majority of cholera deaths worldwide occurred in sub-Saharan Africa.

The World Health Organization (WHO) says that water **sanitation** is key to stopping cholera. Water treatment plants and waste disposal are parts of sanitation. However, these solutions are expensive. Treatment plants can take a long time to build. This is very difficult in remote areas.

Water treatment plants help remove harmful bacteria from a population's water supply.

sanitation—the process of making something clean and free of germs

CHOLERA PREVENTION AND TREATMENTS

Doctors do not use cholera vaccines very often. The vaccine is only approximately 80 to 87 percent effective. Even though the vaccine remains effective for two to three years, some vaccinated people are not protected. This is because the immune system does not have a strong response to the vaccine. Even people who have been vaccinated have to be revaccinated every few years. Otherwise they will no longer be protected.

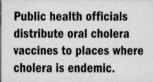

Public health officials distribute oral cholera vaccines to places where cholera is endemic.

ORS packets are mixed into clean drinking water.

If people travel abroad to places where cholera is endemic, they may receive the vaccine. In those cases, vaccines can be up to 90 percent effective. This is because the visitors may also drink bottled water and wash their vegetables with clean water. People who live in areas where cholera is common don't have those options.

The most dangerous part of cholera is dehydration. Once people become severely dehydrated, they are at risk of dying. Rehydration is more important and more effective than antibiotics. Doctors use oral rehydrating solution (ORS). ORS is a mixture of salt and sugars in water. ORS is a drink for patients. People who are very dehydrated may get IV fluids.

THE FUTURE OF CHOLERA

Health officials say that the world is in a seventh cholera pandemic. It began more than 55 years ago. Cholera will continue to affect people in areas where clean water and safe waste disposal are not available. Health officials continue to monitor cholera outbreaks. They provide support in the form of clean water and doctors to assist local clinics and hospitals.

Reducing cholera deaths is very important. WHO created a plan in 2017 to cut the number of deaths by 90 percent. They are hoping to accomplish this goal by 2030.

CHOLERA IN HAITI

In 2010 an earthquake struck Haiti. Much of the country was destroyed. Then another disaster struck. United Nations (UN) aid workers from Nepal brought cholera into the country. Both citizens and officials were unprepared for the rapid spread of the disease. Many organizations didn't have money left after the earthquake. They couldn't help the cholera patients. About 800,000 Haitians were infected with cholera. More than 9,000 people died because of the disease.

However, cholera still infects between 1.3 and 4 million people each year. Of those, 21,000 to 143,000 people die. Health workers and scientists will continue to work to stop the spread of this dangerous infectious disease.

People around the world continue to test water sources for cholera bacteria.

GLOSSARY

bacterium (bak-TEER-eeh-uhm)—a tiny organism that can cause illness

contaminated (con-TAM-ih-nay-ted)—unfit for use because of contact with a harmful substance

dehydrated (dee-HI-dray-ted)—a state of not having enough water

endemic (ehn-DEH-mik)—regularly found in a certain area

epidemic (eh-pih-DEH-mik)—an outbreak of a disease that covers multiple cities

hypothesis (hi-PAH-thih-sis)—an educated guess that can be tested

intravenous (ihn-trah-VEE-nuss)—given through the veins

isolate (EYE-soh-late)—to separate from something else

microorganism (mye-crow-OR-gah-nis-em)—a tiny organism that can only be seen through a microscope

pandemic (pan-DEH-mik)—a worldwide outbreak of an infectious disease

sanitation (san-ih-TAY-shuhn)—the process of making something clean and free of germs

shock (SHOK)—a medical condition caused by a dangerous drop in blood pressure and flow; people suffering from shock can die

trend (TREND)—a pattern in data

vaccine (vak-SEEN)—a substance made up of dead, weakened, or living organisms that is given to a person to protect against a disease

READ MORE

Cummings, Judy Dodge. *Epidemics and Pandemics: Real Tales of Deadly Diseases.* Mystery and Mayhem. Norwich, Vt.: Nomad Press, 2018.

Flynn, Riley. *Water Isn't Wasted! How Does Water Become Safe to Drink?* The Story of Sanitation. North Mankato, Minn.: Capstone Press, 2019.

Rake, Jody Sullivan. *Roots, Bulbs, and Bacteria: Growths of the Underground.* North Mankato, Minn.: Capstone Press, 2016.

INTERNET SITES

Cholera: 10 Killer Facts
http://www.cnn.com/2008/HEALTH/12/03/cholera.facts/index.html

National Institute of Environmental Health Sciences: Epidemiology . . . What's That?
https://kids.niehs.nih.gov/topics/how-science-works/epidemiology/index.htm

TeensHealth: Cholera
https://kidshealth.org/en/teens/cholera.html

INDEX